Achieving
Business
Alchemy
in a week

ROBERT ASHTON

Hodder & Stoughton

A MEMBER OF THE HODDER HEADLINE GROUP

As the champion of management, the
Chartered Management Institute shapes and
supports the managers of tomorrow. By sharing
intelligent insights and setting standards in
management development, the Institute helps
to deliver results in a dynamic world.

chartered

management

institute

inspiring leaders

For more information call 01536 204222 or visit www.managers.org.uk

Orders: please contact Bookpoint Ltd, 130 Milton Park, Abingdon, Oxon
OX14 4SB. Telephone: (44) 01235 827720. Fax: (44) 01235 400454. Lines are open
from 9.00–6.00, Monday to Saturday, with a 24 hour message answering service.
Email address: orders@bookpoint.co.uk

British Library Cataloguing in Publication Data
A catalogue record for this title is available from The British Library

ISBN 0 340 857684

First published   2002
Impression number 10 9 8 7 6 5 4 3 2 1
Year   2007 2006 2005 2004 2003 2002

Typeset by SX Composing DTP, Rayleigh, Essex.
Printed in Great Britain for Hodder & Stoughton Educational, a division of
Hodder Headline Plc, 338 Euston Road, London NW1 3BH. by
Cox & Wyman Ltd, Reading, Berkshire.

'Without Alchemy we would stagnate'

From Charles Handy's *The New Alchemists* photographed by
Elizabeth Handy and published by Hutchinson

C O N T E N T S

It was probably Charles Handy who first used the word alchemist in a management context. In several of his books he wrote about people who have the ability to create something from nothing. He called these people 'new alchemists'.

To become an alchemist you simply have to learn to see things in a new and different way. You have to look for the opportunity in everything you encounter and listen carefully to what people say. Alchemists choose to win without competing and are usually more successful as a result.

This book will help you to use alchemy to create new things. As an alchemist, you will be able to achieve much more than you would otherwise. Alchemy can help you to:

- Make more things happen
- Make budgets go further
- Meet new and interesting people
- Develop your career faster
- Enjoy more of the things you do

What is alchemy?

Today we will explore the concept of alchemy and consider
the opportunity that this technique presents to each of us.
Alchemy virtually eliminates rivalry and makes your ideas
more visible to those who you hope will accept them.

- Discover why alchemy beats rivalry
- Review your life goals
- Consider your career goals
- Refresh your networking skills
- Understand the value of 'hidden' messages

Alchemists often face tremendous opposition because they
dare to challenge the status quo. They indulge in what some
call 'thinking outside the box', or in other words they are
challenging and never take no for an answer. Sometimes,
families, friends and colleagues quite simply cannot see the
opportunity and often ridicule the new idea that the

alchemist has suggested. To be an alchemist, you have to be resilient and explore every avenue before you ever heed the advice of those who say 'it cannot be done'.

Who can be an alchemist?

Anyone can be an alchemist, but some people will find it easier than others. To a large extent, it depends on the sort of person you are and even the amount of freedom you were allowed as a child. Let us look at what makes a good alchemist.

Inquisitive – likes to know how and why things work

Good listener – interprets what is heard

Lateral – happy to use things out of context

Squirrel-like – collects ideas and information for later

Think about the last social gathering you attended. Was there a very loud chap with the florid face who was talking too much? As he continued to drink did he became rather boring? He may have known everyone, but how easy would it be for him to be an alchemist? Pretty difficult, because he did all the talking and will not have heard anything new that he could use. The more likely alchemist would be the person patiently listening while exchanging glances across the room with someone they know, but with whom they have not 'connected' yet at the party. He or she would be polite enough to stay, but independent enough to communicate with other people at the same time.

The job you have been trained to do also has a bearing. People working in finance for example, spend their whole lives focusing on accuracy and detail and may find it harder to apply alchemy than if they worked in a sales environment. To be an alchemist you have to want to be different and, in reality, that is more a state of mind than a product of conditioning, no matter what job you do or who influenced your personal development.

Alchemy versus rivalry

The traditional approach to any challenge is to find someone who has what you want and take it. Rivalry is endemic and while healthy competition can provoke innovation, rivals always look to better what exists, rather than create something new. Rivalry takes place in almost every aspect of the world and is the process by which 'natural selection' allows genetic improvement amongst animals. That is where we learned, as a species, to use rivalry to get our way. Here are some examples to show you what we mean.

Rivalry	Alchemy
• Trying to take what someone already has	• Trying to create something different
• Fighting hard to build market share	• Laying the foundation of a new market
• Applying for a promotion at work	• Proposing a new role at work
• Joining a voluntary organisation	• Starting a voluntary organisation

You can see from the table that the alchemist has to work harder to start with, but once the idea has been developed, the field is relatively clear.

Obviously, it is much harder to think of something without any help. People who have an ambition to work on their own, but no clear business idea, often look at what businesses already exist and set out to compete with the ones that they admire most.

Some ideas for generating ideas

Before alchemy can take place there has to be an idea and usually the starting place for that idea is competitive. In other words, you have seen something that you want that someone else has got already. It could be a job, a client, a car, a house. Let us assume for the sake of simplicity, that you really like cars and are fed up with your ageing hatchback. You have seen people driving new, fast cars and want one too. However, you cannot really afford a new car because you are saving for a holiday, a new kitchen and more besides. Your creative thought process in this instance follows this negative and self-damaging pattern.

> Envy – I want their car
>
> Frustration – I cannot afford it
>
> Self-criticism – if I had won that promotion I could . . .
>
> Defeat – I will never drive a car like that

None of us really want to go through life like this, do we?

Now let us see how someone with alchemist tendencies might approach the same challenge.

Envy – I want their car

Adaptation – I want to drive nice cars

Resource review – I enjoy writing articles for our company newsletter

Networking – I know the editor of our local weekly paper

Alchemy – I could become their motoring writer

Success – I drive and write about a different, nice car every week

Benchmarking – I am more successful because they only drive one nice car

It is really important to focus on exactly what you want. In our example, the turning point is the realisation that it is driving, not owning a nice car that is the goal. Indeed, further thinking will quickly enable you to see that driving the car costs nothing, while owning it (by which we mean paying for the car itself, insurance, servicing and fuel) brings with it expenses that make ownership inaccessible to all but those who can afford the luxury. Having recognised exactly what the objective really is, it is not quite so difficult to review the skills, contacts and other resources that can be exploited to deliver a better result than you first thought possible.

Another important aspect of the alchemy used in this example is that our subject, who now is a part-time motoring correspondent, is not the only beneficiary. The newspaper editor may have been looking for a motoring writer who, by featuring a new car every week, provides new and lucrative opportunities to sell advertising to the dealer who sells the featured models. Both parties benefit from the symbiosis that alchemy delivers. That way, alchemy grows, develops and meets the needs of all concerned.

More ideas for generating more ideas

You have seen from the example of the car enthusiast that setting realistic goals and then setting out to creatively achieve them, enabled the initial ambition to be surpassed.

If you think, you will realise that there is nothing new with this form of 'personal' alchemy. The most contented people I know are those who have made their passion into their job, or at least used alchemy to give them a little of what they know gives them real pleasure. Here are a few more examples:

House sitting – your chance to enjoy the most luxurious accommodation for free

Yacht delivery – sail the finest craft, again at no cost to you

Voluntary work – make an impact in the field that most excites you

In fact, you are probably already thinking of some idea of your own that can make your life more pleasurable. Put this book down for a moment and make a list, remembering of course that alchemy requires the other party to benefit as much from the activity as you do.

Life goals – what are they and why do I need them?

We have seen how you can use alchemy to have fun, and of course we should all strive to make sure that life is pleasurable. However, in some ways the ultimate question is what is life really all about? Now, accepting that this book is neither philosophical nor religious, it is a fairly safe question for me to ask. We are all individuals, physically a product of our parents' genes; that we cannot change. Emotionally, though, we are a product of our parenting, our environment, culture, community and our exposure to things we can aim for. Put simply, it is hard to aspire to things we do not know exist. Nevertheless, we can adapt and develop our ambitions more easily than we can adapt our physiques.

The benefit of setting life goals is that if you know where you are going, you will know when you get there. In other words, if you have decided what you want your life to look and feel like in the future, you will enjoy the satisfaction of having achieved your personal ambitions all the more.

Life goals – how to set them

Here is a technique to introduce you to the concept of life goals. Remember that, now you are going to be an alchemist, many of the things you thought unrealistic will be within your eventual reach. Take a large piece of paper and draw a table like the one below.

In **one** year's time I am	Which means that this year I must
In **two** years' time I am	Which means that this year I must

In **five** years' time I am	Which means that this year I must
In **ten** years' time I am	Which means that this year I must

Now fill in the boxes, always writing your goals in the left-hand column in the present tense to make the goals alive. Then, in the right-hand column write what you have to do over the next year to make those future hopes become reality. For example:

In **one** year's time I am 40. I am earning £40,000 p.a. I live in a new apartment overlooking a harbour. I drive a BMW and have just returned from a holiday in Florida.	Which means that this year I must: • Be promoted to team leader • Start my MBA • Move house • Change my car
In **two** years' time I am 41. I am earning £42,000 p.a. and my new partner and I are expecting our first child.	Which means that this year I must: • Start meeting new people • Develop a social life • Find someone to love

Career goals – what are they and why do I need them?

When you have completed your first draft of your 5-year personal plan, defining life goals and planning your career becomes easier. You will probably have found that your short-term goals are largely materialistic and your long-term goals are more about lifestyle. That is pretty normal, the difference of course is in the detail. Setting goals means knowing what you want your life to look like. It is then much easier to plan how to achieve those goals.

Taking the above example, the short-term goal is to earn more money, take more responsibility and find a partner to share life with. It is quite simple in this scenario to see how undergoing training and developing a wider circle of contacts will help. Using alchemy will help even more, because it will enable more goals to be achieved with everyone benefiting.

Planning career or business goals is the only way you will achieve the way of life you aspire to in the medium to long term.

Career goals – how to set them

The technique for defining your career goals is very similar to that for defining life goals. What is important is that you look at your life goals first. This process will have given you both some goals and the actions needed to achieve them. Take a large piece of paper and draw a second table:

In **one** year's time I am	Which means that this year I must
In **two** years' time I am	Which means that this year I must
In **five** years' time I am	Which means that this year I must

Now fill in the boxes, once again using the present tense, but listing your career goals. While doing this, refer back to your life goals because the two tables you create should be complementary.

In **one** year's time I am 40	Which means that this year I must:
• I am team leader • I work in the export department • I travel widely in my job, meeting lots of new people	• Be promoted to team leader • Start my MBA • Refresh my language skills
In **two** years' time I am 41 • I am still a team leader • I am seconded to 'internal audit' which means that I travel less	Which means that this year I must: • Get to know the audit team • Let people know of my ambition • Delegate effectively to my team

How to win support through alchemy

Having set yourself clear life and career goals for the next few years, it is time to involve other people in the process. It is difficult to think of any life or career path that does not involve influencing other people. The following chapters will introduce you to different kinds of people, all of whom can help you to realise your goals. You might not have considered them all to be of value to you, but if you are to truly succeed you cannot know and understand enough people. Additionally, the more varied the range of contacts you make, the richer your network will become and the more value it will deliver for you.

This is where it might be good to revisit the characteristics that make a good alchemist. Let's explore each one in turn and see how it relates to what we have covered so far.

Inquisitiveness – you cannot be too inquisitive. How does that work? Why is this always done the same way? Who else could benefit? Ask lots of questions.

Listen carefully – often it is what is assumed and not said that is most interesting.

Think laterally – people are a common factor in every field of endeavour, so why can't ideas, concepts, products and tools transfer as readily?

Be squirrel-like – collects ideas and information for later. Carry a notebook and use it.

Who can help you to be an alchemist?

Quite simply, everyone can help you to become an alchemist. One of the skills of a true alchemist is an ability to see an opportunity in everything they encounter. Reflect a moment on our example of the person who wants to drive nice cars, but cannot afford to own one. I always keep in touch with people, however temporarily irrelevant they seem, and often find out about new opportunities.

Here are some pointers that can help you pick out the best people to network with as you develop your skills as an alchemist.

Alchemists – have they got the skill you are currently developing?

Active – are they involved with lots of organisations, both work and social?

Senior – are they far enough up the ladder to make it happen quickly?

Varied – do their own networks stretch and, therefore, extend your own?

Today then, we have looked at:

- What alchemy is and how it can be defined
- How everyone can become an alchemist, if they think in the right way
- How goals can focus your activity as an alchemist
- Who to pick out from the crowd to help you

Applying alchemy to your personal life

Who likes Mondays? The start of a new working week. Pretend that this one is a bank holiday and spend it thinking about ourselves. Reflect for a moment on those goals you set yourself yesterday and ask yourself how you are going to achieve them. Let us spend today looking at how, by using alchemy, you can prepare yourself for the challenges ahead.

- Discover why alchemists get noticed
- Develop your skills as an alchemist
- Things to practise at home
- Techniques for winning in the office
- Appreciate why you should always network

You could be forgiven for feeling a little concerned that, despite having realised that alchemy is a useful technique, it cannot really be applied in your business. However, by the end of today, our metaphorical bank holiday, you will be quite comfortable with some of the basic techniques. We will explore them together and use examples that you can try throughout the day, before returning to your workplace tomorrow. That way, you can build your confidence as an alchemist without any risk.

Spotting the natural alchemist

In a few moments, we will dig into the characteristics that can be found in good alchemists. They are, you will recall, inquisitiveness, alert listening, lateral thinking and an enthusiasm for gathering data and collecting people.

Alchemists all seem to be in the middle of the action. Always in the right place at the right time. The reasons are quite simple, they are there because they have helped create the action that you see is benefiting them. Here are some examples to get you thinking.

Good alchemists

- Make sure they know the right people
- Always volunteer to get involved and help
- Seize opportunities
- Always stay in touch

Of course, sometimes we do not want friends and colleagues from the past to make contact years later, but usually it is welcome. When that call out of the blue is appreciated, the ensuing conversation inevitably highlights shared interests or goals. A good example is that people who sell life insurance are sometimes encouraged to make a list of all the people they know. The fact is that people who know you, or even just remember you from their past, are much more likely to buy from you.

How to be inquisitive without being nosy

To succeed as an alchemist, you have to be aware always of what is around you. You also have to be alive to the opportunities behind the things that you notice. Remember that often there will be no immediate opportunity to exploit the knowledge that you gain, but in time you will soon find it useful. You may feel inhibited about being inquisitive but, with practice and some simple techniques, you will soon be ferreting into everything around you. There is a theory that the brain is like a muscle and that the more you use it, the stronger it becomes. The brain also has tremendous capacity and can happily store all that you discover without becoming overloaded. Do not worry, therefore, about the value of your discoveries; just file them all away. Here are some ways to be inquisitive without appearing to be nosy.

Inquisitive	Nosy
Asking open questions	Asking closed questions
Reading the label on a machine	Reading the label on someone's suit
Watching people in the street	Watching people through their window
Opening closed doors in public buildings	Opening closed doors in a friend's home

A practical benefit of being inquisitive is your response to that great British institution, the queue. Next time you are confronted with a queue, be inquisitive and do not just stand there. Ask how long the queue will last, go for a coffee and try again later or, in a shop, take your purchases to the complaints desk and complain about the queue. You can usually pay there instead.

How to hear what is not said

We are conditioned as children to listen to what is said. We all sat in school eagerly hearing and often writing down the words that the teacher uttered, but we forget to listen to what is not said. In terms of alchemy, the opportunity is often revealed by what is not said, rather than by what is actually said. Sales people are perhaps the best at picking up these hidden messages, but we can all benefit from listening more efficiently. Moreover, you do not have to guess at the hidden message; ask the right question and it will be revealed to you.

> **Q** – Why is there not a 25 per cent reduction on this jacket?
>
> **A** – that item is not in the sale, Sir.
>
> **Q** – So what discount can you give me?
>
> **A** – I suppose I could give you 15 per cent.

Those of us who are not alchemists would have paid the full price or walked away. Rather like the queue we talked about a moment ago, people who explore more than their peers, get more than their peers.

Thinking laterally

Much has been written about lateral thinking and, indeed, people like Edward de Bono have made their name by writing books on the subject. A simple way to look at lateral thinking is to never take no for an answer. That is, to recognise there is usually a solution to the problem, but that it is not an obvious solution. Often, solutions can be found in a different place to where you are looking. Most business sectors never look beyond their boundaries for new ideas, and make matters worse by only recruiting people with knowledge and experience gained within that sector.

A company that runs many business events and conferences uses a database developed for arts venues. Furthermore, they also hired a marketing manager from the arts sector. The lateral thought that sparked their decision was the recognition that even the most serious, heavyweight business conference must be entertaining and enjoyable if people are to return the next year. They looked at how their local theatre managed the process and decided to do the same.

Lateral thinking

- Never accept no; always seek alternatives that deliver a win:win
- Look for parallel solutions in sectors different to your own
- Try mind mapping™ as a way of exploring alternatives on paper
- Persist and do not be swayed by those around you who wish to give up!

Building your people collection

Alchemy needs people and, rather like knowledge, you cannot have too much or too many. The fault that most people make is only to make contact when they want something or they can see some other immediate benefit from getting in touch. This is, unfortunately, the reason why most people struggle with their challenges and do not find ready solutions. If you accept that all people are useful to know, the problem is only how to build and manage your network. Building your network is simple.

- Meet more people by joining things and getting to know those you meet
- Use contact management software to store relevant facts and to give you prompts
- Be different when keeping in touch. Send New Year, not Christmas cards!
- Help other people first, they will then help you later
- Ask people for introductions to people who can help you

Applying alchemy at home

Before using alchemy at work, it is always a good idea to practise at home. Indeed, there are real benefits to applying alchemy to your home life. For example:

- Your home budget probably needs to go further than your budget at work
- You can benefit those you care about most; your family
- It is safer to practise on family and friends than on your colleagues at work

Perhaps one of the best examples of alchemy in the home is the babysitting circle. Think about it. People do not often live near their parents or siblings nowadays, and finding babysitters can be a real challenge. One person decides that to face the challenge individually is rather pointless and gets together a group of parents to create a babysitting circle. The result? Everyone finds it easier to go out in the evening. An extension of this concept is the Local Exchange Trading Systems (LETS) schemes that are emerging in many communities. Here, the same principle is applied, except that a wider range of skills and resources are offered. So one person who has a chain-saw might cut logs for a neighbour, who pays with 'credits' which can then be redeemed against a service that he needs, perhaps help with his computer.

Think now about the community that you live in. Are there opportunities to create sharing schemes in your locality?

Alchemy further afield

Another superb example of alchemy is the 'house swap'.
People have recognised the simple fact that when you are
away on holiday, you are not at home! In other words, you
do not need your home when you go away for a fortnight, so
why not save on hotel bills and swap houses with someone
who lives where you want to spend your holiday? Agencies
have sprung up to handle the necessary introductions, and
you can tour each other's homes on websites and get to know
each other by e-mail before actually swapping houses.

Make a list of the ways that you could use alchemy to
improve your life at home. The table below lists a few ideas
to get you started.

- Set up an 'equipment' swap scheme in your street or
  village
- Create a 'lift sharing' network to save fuel and
  improve commuting
- Start a dining club, each couple hosting in turn

Think about how your list will:

- Improve your life and the lives of those around you
- Save people money through cooperation and
  sharing
- Improve the environment, perhaps through fuel
  saving

Think too of the personal benefits that can accrue from applying alchemy in your local community.

- Recognition as an innovator, someone who makes things happen
- A wide circle of contacts
- Valuable material to add to your CV

Using alchemy to develop yourself

We all know that a business's biggest asset (and usually its biggest cost) is the people who work there. This never seems to make it easier to find the budget for training and development, but alchemy can help you. Although this chapter is really about practising alchemy at home, some of the best opportunities for learning and self-development are available out of the workplace. What you will find is that the words used to describe these opportunities are different and, often, the provider of what we will call 'off the job' training does not fully appreciate what they have to offer.

Many of our larger organisations have recognised the opportunities for learning that exist out of work. For example, board members of some of the UK's largest companies are actively encouraged to take non-executive directorships in smaller, non-competing companies. This enables them to broaden their skills and prevents them from getting too 'locked in' to their own organisational culture. You may not be a director of a major plc, but this does not stop you from building your knowledge, skills and experience in a similar way.

Free training for you

As you will have guessed, perhaps, community involvement can deliver new skills, build confidence and enable you to help others too. In fact, the social economy is growing quickly as more people choose to work full-time in an environment where financial return on capital is not the prime motivator. We have talked about how, as an alchemist, you can create new organisations such as babysitting circles. But there is a lot more to be gained. For example:

Management training	Become a school Governor or a charity trustee
Leadership/people management	Help with young people's groups, scouts, guides etc.
Mentoring/ coaching	Be a business mentor with the Princes Trust Work with young ex-offenders to develop their basic skills
Interviewing	Provide interview experience to sixth formers

You may feel that volunteering to help others is not the best way to train yourself, but there are a number of people for whom this is the only way to experience some aspects of management. Quite simply, their current jobs do not provide the opportunities. What is more, when applying for promotion jobs, they will score over their rivals because they have proof of competence through involvement in organisations outside work.

Using alchemy in the workplace

So, having practised alchemy at home, we can now start to think about how to apply it at work. We can spend the rest of today looking at personal opportunities and then tomorrow move on with confidence to corporate alchemy.

Alchemy can bring about real changes in the workplace at all levels. Staying with the theme of training and development, the opportunity to share resources with other businesses is tremendous. Imagine that you manage a small call centre where ten people answer telephone calls from the public. Next door is a company that fits windscreens and, around the corner, a builders' merchant. Each company is quite small, but collectively has 20 people in customer facing roles. Together, you could buy two training sessions in, say, customer care, each sending half of your team on each day, ensuring that work continued back at base. Through collaborating and applying some alchemy to your business you gain in several ways.

Training delivered locally	Staff away from the workplace for less time
'In-house' programme	Lower cost than places on 'open' programme Training tailored to your needs
Delegates from three companies	People learn from the experience of others
Encourages networking	More opportunities for sharing can be explored

The same principle can be applied across a spectrum of business activity, making possible some of the small, but important things that big organisations take for granted.

Creating a community at work

We talked earlier about the value of community involvement in meeting personal development and training needs. The same principles can apply in the workplace. In other words, in an organisation of 100 people, you have a community representing perhaps more than 300 people, assuming that most have partners and children. Think what you can achieve for these people if you apply a little alchemy. Consider the benefits to the organisation if its people feel that they are part of a work-based community, where the whole family can take part in activities. An example is coach operators who regularly put together package holidays for factory workers who, odd as it may seem, enjoy the chance to holiday together during the summer shut-down. Day trips at the weekend are excellent for team-building and for developing loyalty to the business, even though they take place at the weekend and are not usually subsidised. Many employers overlook the opportunity to team-build, using their team's own time and money!

Make a list of things that you could organise for your colleagues and their families. Then create a plan to put them into action.

Summary

Today we have explored how alchemy can make a difference to your life. Not just to your home life, although that aspect is important, but to you as an individual at work. We have gained an understanding of how alchemists get noticed because they tend to achieve so much more than everyone else. We have also begun to practise the art of alchemy in a safe environment and thought about some examples where alchemy can make a difference at work.

Perhaps now would be a good time to brush up on your networking skills because, by now, you will have realised that alchemy is all about influencing people and bringing them together to join in the activities that you have chosen.

Here then are some networking techniques for you to remember:

Objective	Activity
Meeting new people	Join organisations, networks and clubs.
Starting conversations	Essential if networking is to take place. At all the best events people are given clear, legible name badges. Catch the person's eye and ask an opening question like, 'Tell me, what does ABC Engineering do?'

Finding things out	Ask open questions. These cannot be answered 'yes' or 'no'. For example, 'How has the Euro affected you?'
Checking understanding, gaining agreement	Ask closed questions. For example, 'So, if we organised that training at our place, you'd send people along?'
Staying in touch	If the person has potential to add value to your network, make sure you agree to do something after the meeting. Perhaps e-mail an article or contact to them or perhaps even meet again.
Making it easy	Contact management software can help the most active networker to keep in touch and keep personal – you can record the facts you might otherwise forget.

Using alchemy in a business context

So far we have practised alchemy at home, in our local community and used the technique to accelerate our personal development and training. Now it is time to apply alchemy to our business. Of course, much of what we have covered so far will benefit your organisation. As an alchemist, you are a more resourceful manager, able to save money through building successful partnerships. However, the most powerful way to apply your emerging new skill is in your organisation's marketplace. Today, we will consider:

- Who your customers actually are
- What they really need from you
- How to focus on value rather than cost
- How to add share opportunities
- Building customer loyalty and commitment

Do not assume that you have to be in a customer facing role to use alchemy effectively. We have already seen how an organisation can benefit from sharing resources and training with neighbours. Today we focus on the customer because, in most commercial organisations, the customer provides the revenue that funds all that the organisation does.

Who is the customer?

When you listen to 'experts' on organisational change, they will tell you that everyone is a customer. This philosophy has given rise to the phenomenon of the 'internal marketplace', which can create a quasi-competitive environment in even the most staid public sector organisation. Unfortunately, sometimes the concept gets taken too far and the true customer, the person who ultimately pays, is overlooked because they are harder to please than colleagues in the next office who might represent an internal customer. It is often difficult to see who the true customer is. Here are some thoughts about who your customers might be.

Sector	Examples	Possible customers
Business-to-business	Builders' merchant	Builders (but also some consumers doing DIY)
	Printer	Any business (but also, perhaps, writers)
Business-to-consumer	Insurance broker	The public (but also, perhaps, businesses)
	Garden centre	The public, also, possibly, car showrooms
Government-to-consumer	DVLA	All vehicle owners, individual and corporate
	Social services	Members of the public with particular needs
Health-to-consumer	GP practice	Patients, businesses buying health screening
		The Primary Care Trust who funds them
Education-to-consumer	Schools	Children, but also parents and the local authority who funds them

As you can see, it is not always as straightforward as we might like to make it!

Needs or wants?

In rather the same way that we talked on Sunday about the merits of alchemy over rivalry, the same argument can be applied to needs and wants. Alchemy can only really add value if it is applied to meeting needs. Wants are something quite different. You have to ask the right questions and do not take what you are hearing at face value. Below are some scenarios to show you what we mean.

Wants	Needs
What the customer says they need	What the customer actually needs
'I want a paint that means I never have to paint my windows again'	What the customer really needs is new windows with PVCu frames.
'I only want you to print me 100 brochures as my product range keeps changing'	Printers usually need to produce at least 500 copies to be economic. The customer needs something more flexible, perhaps a website.
'I've got to find an easier way to calculate my staff wages – it's taking me too long to work out at the moment'	While the customer might be asking for software, he still has to find time. He really needs a bureau payroll service.

An immediate challenge in these examples is that what your prospective customer actually needs, may not be the product or service you can offer him or her. You seem to be faced with a simple choice. Sell what you have, or send him to a rival who can provide what is really needed. Think again. If you think laterally and use a little alchemy, you can make an introductory commission from your former rival. Your customer wins, because their needs are met. You make a margin and your new associate gains a customer.

Adding value and reducing cost

In the same way that your customers needs may not necessarily be the same as the things they say they want, so their perception of value may differ from actual cost. A good example of a business that sells on the basis of value alone is an estate agent. By charging a percentage of the sale price, income is not linked to the amount of work involved, but to the value of the property to the customer. This charging basis is one of the reasons that estate agents are not always popular because, while the price is linked to performance, the value is not always clearly seen.

Looking at your organisation, what are the things that your customers value, but that you take for granted? Are you throwing away things you could sell, or at least derive some benefit from?

Delivery	Would some customers pay more for 'same day' delivery? Simply route your truck to go there first!
Hot water	Power stations have sold the hot water used to cool reactors to adjacent growers who use it to heat glasshouses.
Beer	A brewery in Suffolk fattens pigs with the waste beer that would otherwise be thrown away.
Paper	Several printers give their paper off-cuts to local schools. Parents know this and may use the printer.

Recognising and exploiting these opportunities is a way of adding value and saving cost which, as we know, can contribute to profitability.

Selling to new types of customer

We have seen that organisations do not usually have just one customer group. Many consumer businesses also have business customers and so on. Although it is vital to focus on the core business in any enterprise, alchemy can often be used to exploit the peripheral markets. In the last recession, builders' merchants found, not surprisingly, that because fewer houses were being built, their market shrank. Some tried to take market share from the DIY sector, but few managed to do this effectively. Consumers were reluctant to order from a counter and reveal their lack of knowledge when, in a DIY store, they can browse and choose what they want from the product description printed on the packaging. That was consumer perception. The reality was that those people behind the counter could offer free expert advice, help consumers select the right product and deliver bulky items to their door at no extra cost. Both consumers and builders' merchants lose out.

Take a look at your own organisation. Make a list of the customer groups you service well, and perhaps those you currently miss out. Ask yourself these three questions about the sector you do not target at the moment:

- How do their expectations differ from those of my core customers
- How must our products or services be presented/packed to meet their needs?
- What will they pay most for and why?

Using alchemy to sell new things to old customers

It is frustrating when customers do not seem to realise how businesses develop. They keep buying the same old products and services and rarely take advantage of what is new. This is often because we do not do enough to challenge their perceptions about our organisation. Couple this with the fact that it is always more glamorous to chase new customers than sell more to old ones, and you can see why it happens.

Alchemy, remember, is all about creating something new and, in this context, we need to create a new way to introduce your customers to new ideas. For instance, a garage could offer its customers car valeting when they service their car. This is a way of selling more time and value to the customer and, therefore, increasing profit. Other opportunities include:

Opportunity	Benefit
Create customer clubs	Encourages product referral between customers
Customer competitions	Encourages customers to innovate on your behalf
Create 'user group'	Users provide help to each other rather than asking you

Pass the customer

People tend to be overly protective of their customers and always seem reluctant to share them. Yet, in reality, customers belong to no one and no one company can not sell them everything that they want to buy. Moreover, effective collaboration or alchemy, can make life better for customers and suppliers alike. Large organisations do this rather well, with motorway service stations and airports being good examples. These are often packed with retail outlets which pay handsomely for the opportunity to sell to a captive market. Smaller businesses can do this as well, but again alchemy is needed to bring together the participants and to overcome the natural suspicion that many small business owners have. Here is a simple check-list that you can use for your business.

Opportunity	Example
Where could people come from, already excited about your product?	People buy more music CDs when they have just purchased a new sound system. CD shops could have vouchers in hi-fi shops offering an incentive.
What would enhance the performance of your product?	If you are an accountant, your clients would benefit from using the same software as you. Why not introduce them to a supplier?
Why will people keep coming back for more?	Some pig feed companies provide the pigs too. They also buy back the pigs later. They work with associates to minimise risk and build loyalty.
Who else would like my customer?	Tourist attractions place reciprocal discount offers in each other's attractions. It means that whoever gets the first visit, encourages a visit to a second.

| **When** are people most interested in your offer? | Makers of baby products collaborate to deliver 'collections' of products to maternity wards. |

Sharing the journey

We have looked at how to cooperate with other individual businesses to add value to an offer and to make it easier for both to pick up new customers. Think how much more you could achieve if you collaborated with a larger number of other businesses. In a retail environment, this is what happens all the time; people visit a particular shopping centre because of the choice of outlets they know they will find. This is why new retail developments are always so keen to attract the major players; they know that this will bring in the visitors and benefit all of the tenants.

The conference company I spoke about earlier used the same principle when asked to promote a piece of business 'best practice' which, in itself, is unlikely to draw a crowd. What they do is invite interesting speakers from exciting companies to speak at the same events. The offer becomes more appealing, people attend, they hear the 'best practice' speaker and also hear how this has been applied by the supporting speaker's companies. For example, a presentation on the importance of E-commerce might be supported by a budget airline that takes most of its bookings online, and by a web company able to give you the support you need to emulate the airline's success.

This can be called the 'omnibus' effect because participating companies:

- Share the cost of reaching the audience
- Have products and services that fit together in a logical way
- Together add appeal and interest, encouraging more people to attend
- All, therefore, benefit from sharing the journey

Let us look at how this can benefit you.

Building an omnibus campaign

Now it is your turn to achieve this form of alchemy for your organisation. It does not matter what sector you are in, your customers will all benefit and so will you. Also remember where we looked at types of businesses and saw that often there are different groups of customers. A school, for example, can count children, parents and the local education authority as three quite distinct customer groups. Look at your organisation and ask yourself the following questions:

- What audience do I want to reach?
- Who already has access to that audience – or will grab their attention?
- Who can add value to my offer or make it more appealing?
- How can we link our products and services in a unique way?
- How can we reach the market, save money and multiply the effect?

You will be surprised at how receptive most people are to an invitation to take part in an omnibus campaign. After all, we are all looking for a unique way to reach new customers that does not cost the earth. Here are a few more ideas to get you started.

Participants	Opportunity
Hotel, dress shop, hairdresser	Fashion show
Van hire, packaging company, estate agent	DIY home removals
Newspaper, industrial property owner, local authority	Business exhibition
Tourist attractions, hotels, leisure centres	Annual tourist guidebook

Building a Trojan horse

An alternative way of sharing the journey to market is to build a Trojan horse. You will remember the story of the invading army who made, then hid in, a wooden horse. Their enemy took a liking to the horse and, unwittingly, gave the victors fast-track access to their prize. You can do the same, using this particular form of business alchemy.

In this version, we use a metaphorical Trojan horse because few prospective clients will guard their order book with the same zeal as those ancient sentries. The effect, however, is just the same and is a particularly powerful way for small businesses to sell to large ones.

Here is what you need to do.

Feature	Example
Select the offer	Customer care training
Identify target	Local authority
Research opportunity	Performance targets set goals for customer care
Recruit your Trojan horse	Publication read by local authority senior managers
Create opportunity	Offer to survey and benchmark sample of authorities
Exploit opportunity	• Approach authorities using publication's name to get meeting • Offer to give individual feedback afterwards • Publication of your report positions you as an authority and makes selling easier • Publication wins as exclusive report

A simpler example is to appoint a caravan site owner as a distributor for your bottled gas. He then persuades his captive audience to buy your gas. In every case, you gain access to new customers because you are being endorsed by someone they are comfortable with.

Getting customers to do the selling

One of the challenges we all meet is the resistance that inevitably results from you, the supplier, suggesting the opportunity. One way for alchemy to get around this dilemma is by creating a business network to meet the development needs of your target audience. What this does is put the onus on your customers and prospects to help each other. If what you have to offer genuinely helps to achieve this you, as lead sponsor, will inevitably benefit.

My own company did this a few years ago, setting up an entrepreneurs' network in Norfolk, where we are based. We won a government grant to set the network up and to use our facilitating role to gain access to and influence those we wish to work for. It is perhaps important to appreciate that setting up networks is not easy and is, in fact, a long-term investment. This is what you need:

Members	People who benefit from belonging. Many should be your clients.
Sponsors	Non-competing organisations wishing to influence your members. Often can be persuaded to pay to enable events etc. to happen.
Supporters	Usually are publicly funded to help your audience. For example, business support agencies, universities and even some charities.
Publicists	Never forget to include your local/trade press. They spread the word for you, avoiding the need for expensive advertising.

Building a programme of events creates countless opportunities for you, your sponsors and supporters to have constructive, focused contact with the members. What is more, providing that the knowledge content is of a high quality, you will find that the network can become self-financing.

Summary

Today we have focused on the commercial side of business alchemy, discussing how it can be used to add value to your organisation's customer offer. We have also looked at how alchemy can reduce your marketing costs. We are all taught to compete from a very early age, and the drive to increase competitiveness is vital if our nation's small businesses are to prosper. However, reflect for a moment on where that competition really comes from. The plain facts of supply and demand mean that in many UK industries there is enough business to go round, with rivals fighting for marginal business. The threat is not from those we perhaps already know and who trade in the same town, belong to the same trade association, or share the same suppliers. The business rivals who can cause a real problem are those who operate in countries where labour costs are lower and, often, technology is more advanced.

Ask yourself these questions and act on the answers before we move on and look at how business alchemy can benefit other aspects of your organisation.

Alchemy in education

Yesterday we looked at how alchemy can be used to reduce needless competition and can also help you to build strong partnerships with other businesses. Today we take a look at the education sector, which is often underestimated by the business community. Schools are, for most people, simply the places where children are sent to be taught. In reality, however, they are much more. Schools are major employers, often have multi-million pound annual budgets and are under increasing pressure to link with their local business community. The emphasis is to create a stimulating environment within which children will learn through exploration and experience. For the business alchemist, this creates countless opportunities. Today we shall consider those opportunities and in particular will take a look at:

- What is the opportunity?
- Culture, and how schools differ from business
- Existing initiatives that could benefit you
- How your staff can learn at school too
- How schools can make your business more competitive
- Special opportunities for special people

The education opportunity

Education has certainly changed since I went to school. Those of you who are parents may be already involved with your childrens' school, but have you stopped to consider what more you could achieve for both your organisation and your local school with a little alchemy? Let us start by de-mystifying some of that education jargon.

Jargon	Relates to ages	And means
Key stage 1	5–7	Nursery, primary and first schools
Key stage 2	7–11	Primary and middle schools
Key stage 3	11–14	Middle and high schools
Key stage 4	14–16	High school – ends with GCSEs

Further education	16–18	High school, sixth form centre or college, leads to A levels (academic) or GNVQ (vocational)
Higher education	18+	University or college usually leads to HND, degree

The key stages relate to the national curriculum and for each stage there are standard levels of attainment that students are expected to have reached. These are tested at ages 7 and 11 through school assessed tests (SATS), with older children taking formal exams. Schools are tested every few years through an inspection process called OFSTED (the Office for Standards in Education). One measure of success is involvement with business.

The culture of education

It is far too easy to be critical of the education system. However, as an alchemist you must adopt a more positive stance. You will recognise that your opportunity is to help schools and their teachers to overcome the challenges they face, for in return, they will help you to overcome yours. That, after all, is what alchemy is all about.

However, it is fair to say that the worlds of business and education are both structured in such a way that there is very little crossover between them. Nevertheless, in reality education is no different from any other business sector, where young people choose their career, train, develop and gain experience. The difference is that teachers practise their art in the very places where they were trained, limiting their experience of the world outside. In common with most professions, the best practitioners become managers and new head teachers often find themselves ill-equipped to manage the large and complex organisations they are leading.

Priorities are the same in both education and business, but different terminology makes translation sometimes difficult.

Schools	Businesses
Making the budget stretch far enough	Making a profit
Competing to win more students	Competing to win more customers
Developing and retaining staff	Developing and retaining staff
Work experience for students	Supervision experience for staff
Recruit governors with business skills	Management development
Buying inputs at competitive prices	Buying inputs at competitive prices
Being innovative within curriculum boundaries	Being innovative within market boundaries

Making time to do alchemy

It is difficult for those of us working within the business community to sometimes recognise that teachers do work hard. And they really do. While the children are only at school for a few hours a day and for around 40 weeks a year, we tend to forget that teachers have to prepare their lessons, mark exercises, arrange extra-curricular programmes and also find time for personal and career development. Curriculum changes and a growing, national shortage of teachers increases the pressure. So why mention this? Simply because to make alchemy work between businesses and schools, you have to understand the teachers' viewpoint. They, for example, believe that businesses are more sophisticated and better managed than schools and have more choice in how they spend their time.

In fact, both school managers and business managers are busy people and, for alchemy to work, it needs to be focused, effective and relevant to both. Here are a few pointers to help you build the relationship that can allow alchemy to take place.

- Take an interest in the performance of your local schools – easy if your children go there, equally important if you do not have children.
- Allow the school to visit your business; discuss with teachers areas of common interest.
- Invite your local head teacher to a business networking event to build his or her network of contacts. If you can, invite them to be the speaker.

> • Read and appreciate the current drivers for change in education. An hour or so of internet research will make sure that you understand the benefits schools can obtain.

Now that you are better tuned in to the school culture, it is time to start a little alchemy.

Here are some we prepared earlier

As we have said, there is an increasing focus on building effective links between schools and their surrounding business community. To help this happen, an array of publicly funded and not-for-profit organisations have been set up. Each is charged with helping schools to engage effectively with the business community and, because they are all separately funded, they vie against each other for your attention and support. Inevitably, in the presence of so many options, it is difficult to choose which, if any, to support. It is also inevitable that, unless you are a strong business alchemist, you will overlook the simple fact that you can of course design your own project. Here are a few examples:

Work experience	Usually arranged by the local careers service, but sometimes arranged by the school. Involves placing students at key stage 4 (14–16) with an employer for a week or two in early summer.

Young Enterprise *http://www.young-enterprise.org.uk*	Runs a number of initiatives, the most popular being where groups of young people create a business with the help of a business mentor.
Business in the Community (BITC) *http://www.bitc.org.uk*	A diverse organisation working across many sectors. Their 'Partners in Leadership' programme pairs a head teacher with a senior business leader.

How these tool-kits can help you

First, of course, you must know what you want to achieve for yourself and your organisation. Many of the invitations you receive will encourage you to act philanthropically. The benefits to you, however, must at least equal the benefit to the school or the activity will not be sustainable. Let us look at the kinds of needs that can be met through working with schools.

Business need	**Possible activity**
Boost staff morale	Almost any school activity can help
Build staff confidence	Supervising work experience students is an ideal starting point for those with no people management responsibility
Refresh management skills	Mentor a Young Enterprise team, revisiting basic principles with them

Challenge your management thinking and problem solving skills	Mentor and be mentored by a head teacher through BITC

People alchemy with schools

If your business is an Investor in People and hopefully even if it is not, your organisation will have a training plan. This should start with your commercial goals and set out how the people you have will be developed to achieve those goals. Schools also have people development plans and these are usually linked to how the school delivers the national curriculum. All schools and many businesses have training budgets. We talked earlier in the week about how neighbouring companies can share training, reducing the cost, increasing the focus and enabling participants to learn from each other. Think how much more powerful this could be if you also invite your local schools to take part as well. This is also an excellent way to get to know each other as organisations. Schools can also be encouraged to reciprocate. They often allocate their training days to sessions covering both hard and soft skills. Ask yourself whether your staff could benefit from joining sessions on subjects like stress management, first aid and dealing with difficult people. Why not be an alchemist and do the following:

- Map out what training is planned by local businesses and schools
- Broker the 'trading' of participants between organisations, filling empty seats
- Consider together how much more you could afford if sharing the cost
- Make sure you all review the benefits resulting from the training
- Celebrate success together. An annual get-together and awards for the individuals who have gained or contributed the most

People alchemy with children

We have talked about working with school staff, but we must not overlook the fact that schools exist to benefit young people. Business alchemy that brings your staff and children together can be particularly rewarding. Rewarding in terms of the benefits to both organisations, but also in terms of the buzz we all get from helping children to learn and grow. This is where you can be really creative in applying your developing skill as an alchemist. Start by looking at what you and your local school might be seeking to achieve.

School needs	Businesses benefit
Recruit speaker from local business	Staff experience of speaking to groups
Support with reading for slow learners	Raise staff members' self-esteem
Visits to see how businesses work	Engender staff pride through hosting
Work experience for students	Supervision experience for staff
Recruit governors	Exposure to fresh challenges

Again, think about your team and their individual needs. Could they be best met by working with a local school? Helping your people to feel successful, valued and worthwhile will pay handsome dividends. Can you see how, by helping schools, you can gain a competitive edge over others in your market? Remember too, that school staff will often benefit from the opportunity to direct their skills at your challenges. You will be surprised by how well it works when you create your own alchemy with a local school.

Getting competitive at school

You may remain a little sceptical about whether all of your business issues can be dealt with through alchemy. Of course, we all have competitors and rivals who choose to confront us 'head on' in our marketplaces. So far, we have advocated alchemy as an alternative to rivalry, but we shall now look at how alchemy can increase your competitiveness when rivalry cannot be avoided. Once again schools have a role to play, as do colleges and universities. You may not appreciate, for example, that whereas university research grants used to be awarded simply on the merit of the project, many now need a business involvement to get funding. This is because it is recognised that the real value of knowledge only results from its application. In other words, you can enhance a university's reputation and earning power if you allow their academics to help you to gain a market advantage.

Conveniently, there are a number of ready-made alchemy solutions just sitting on the shelf waiting for you. That is, unless your competitors get there first! Here are some examples.

Opportunity	Which means
High schools can win additional funding to become 'specialist schools', focusing on either Technology, Engineering, Science, Maths & Computing, Sports, Arts, Language, Business & Enterprise	When successful, they will have the resources and desire to use your business challenges as study material for their students.

Teaching company scheme *www.tcsonline.org.uk*	A DTI (Department of Trade and Industry) funded programme that gets you a graduate working full-time for 2 years on a specific project in your business. Salary, academic support, training and IT heavily subsidised.

Making magic with special people

One group of schools often overlooked by businesses seeking to build partnerships and 'do alchemy' are the so called 'special schools'. These are schools where children with special needs are educated. With high staff to pupil ratios, lots of specialist equipment and substantial budgets, these schools work with children who cannot easily integrate into mainstream education. Children at special schools may have either physical or learning disabilities and they are streamed according to the severity of the challenge they face. Alchemy with special schools has to be undertaken with a high degree of sensitivity, but can be very rewarding in many ways.

Consider for a moment, some of the opportunities for your team to benefit from working alongside a special school.

School needs	Your opportunity
Additional funding for specialist equipment and staff	Support the school with fund-raising and team-building activities: • Demonstrates that you are a caring company • Broadens staff understanding • Can strengthen customer/supplier links
Simple, classroom projects	Enable members of your team to work in the classroom, perhaps demonstrating work practices. This can be very rewarding for staff.
Sharing resources	There may be opportunities to share skills, equipment and more with a local special school.

Why not visit a special school yourself and see what can be achieved through business alchemy?

Summary

We have seen today that there are tremendous opportunities to develop business alchemy with schools. To really benefit, you need to consider building a long-term relationship, with activity at all levels. This can create a 'twinning' atmosphere between your organisation and the school, with your people contributing to and benefiting from the relationship.

Before we move on from education, let us review the benefits for you and your organisation of working with a school.

Save money	Many of the activities we have talked about will meet your training needs without you spending cash.
Build confidence	School links create opportunities for 'people supervision' for all, even those at the bottom of the organisation. All who participate will feel valued and needed.
Positive PR	Given the choice, we would all work for and with organisations that care. This alchemy demonstrates caring.
Opens minds	Exposure to the challenges facing young people with learning disabilities gives people a new perspective on life and their personal values. Open-minded people will always achieve more, both at work and in their lives.

020000 048572 020

How to develop winning partnerships with voluntary organisations

Yesterday we explored how alchemy can enable your organisation to benefit from school liaisons. Today we visit the voluntary sector, which is perhaps underestimated to an even greater extent by the business community. One of the big challenges for you to meet, as an alchemist, is the breadth of the voluntary sector and the fact that, rather like education, the people talk a different language from the language of business.

Charities are closely regulated by the Charities Commission and this both provides constraints and creates opportunities. Additionally, there is regulation surrounding the establishment, operation and taxation of charities. In this chapter we shall look at some of the things you can do to advance your organisation through alchemy with the voluntary sector. However, what this book cannot do, is provide specific advice on any of the legal aspects of relationships with charities. Your accountant and solicitor would be good people to check with before embarking on anything substantial in this sector.

Having voiced a few words of caution, let us see where we can go today. We will explore the following areas:

- What is the voluntary sector?
- Small things that are easy to do
- A unique style of product placement
- Ready-made opportunities
- Broadening management experience
- How to entertain your customers for free

How to define the voluntary sector

At the risk of being considered controversial, we will include a wide variety of activities within this section. This is because we are talking about alchemy and need to include situations that create opportunity. As with education, you need to be sensitive to the feelings of your team before dragging them into a cause they might not identify with. Indeed, one of the joys of the diversity of this sector is that people can engage with organisations and causes that they do really believe in. The resulting resonance will build commitment and guarantee mutual success. Moreover, people learn more when involved in projects they enjoy. Here is a segmentation of the voluntary sector.

Group	Example
Local campaign	Project to equip a children's playground
Arts project	Many theatres and some cinemas are set up as charities

Local charity	Often run by a passionate founder, can deal with all kinds of issues including health, environment, historic buildings
National charity	High profile, national organisations, often with local fund-raisers and branches
National campaign	Annual, high profile events that raise cash, for example, 'Children in Need'
Global charities	Organisations as varied as Oxfam and Greenpeace

Before going further, you need to appreciate that fund-raising is a profession, practised with great dexterity by the larger organisations. For alchemy to work, you have to make sure that you are going to benefit as well.

Avoiding common pitfalls

It is horribly easy when you are busy to fall for one of the following schemes which are heavily promoted by specialist companies.

Scheme	Reality
Buying advertising in charity diaries, wall planners and celebratory brochures	Too little of your donation goes to the good cause and few of your customers will see the advertising.
Collecting tins in your office reception area	If you believe in the cause, donate £10 and do not let the tin clutter your office. It can send confusing messages to customers and staff.
Get sponsored to trek/cycle in exotic location	Essentially a fund-raising holiday and should be treated as such.

Alchemy is all about making something new happen, with your organisation and another benefiting from something worthwhile. From experience, the examples above do not constitute alchemy and, in almost all cases, given time and effort you can achieve more if you think first.

Putting the opportunity into perspective

As with any business decision, you need to distinguish between emotion and logic, personal fascination and collective team interest. It is particularly difficult to retain focus and objectivity when working with the voluntary sector. To start you practising alchemy, consider the question of fit. What I mean is the link, actual or perceived, between your organisation and the one you are planning to collaborate with. Ask yourself these questions.

Question	Example
To what extent does this campaign reach people I would like to influence?	A motor dealer can gain by getting involved in a road safety campaign.
Can the benefits help my organisation?	A local factory landscapes the park where many of its workers' children play.
What new knowledge and skills will we acquire?	A hotel teams up with a hostel for the homeless to share training resources.

You will see from the examples that, in many cases, there will be a clear link between your organisation's involvement and the benefits you gain. Naturally, they will be harder to define than perhaps a straight commercial transaction, but the cost will be lower too. As previously mentioned, often the greatest benefits of alchemy are the soft benefits. People want to work with organisations that practise alchemy.

If you try to work out how to ensure that the projects you become involved with will benefit you, you should, by now, be able to do so straight away. To get the greatest benefit, you have to take the initiative and start the project yourself. That is what true alchemists do.

Small things to get you started

Throughout this book, in each aspect of alchemy, we have used some simple examples to get you started. Here is a simple but effective example. It is quite simple, but proved to be really effective.

A charity that provides residential accommodation and training for single homeless people was finding it difficult to make people realise that the charity had evolved to become much more than just a night shelter and soup kitchen. People were happy to put a pound in a collecting tin or to send unwanted bedding. What the organisation really wanted was volunteers to help residents to rebuild their self-respect. A local design company produced a brochure for the organisation that contained posed portraits of homeless people and told their stories. This enabled the charity to challenge public perceptions about homelessness; people could see that homeless people were just like anyone else. The design company, on the other hand, now had a stunning example of creativity to show their commercial clients. Both organisations won.

Make a list of the things that your organisation could do to get started in this field. When you have made the list, discuss it with your colleagues. Make a plan and follow it!

Making your products do alchemy

Those involved with marketing will know that the most successful products are those that are strongly branded. In other words, the brand or product identity conveys in a very clear way the benefits that the product can deliver its users. This brand personality or set of values is strongly identified with by the consumer. For example, which motor manufacturer focuses hardest on safety? The answer of course is that they all do, but you may have thought of the one in Sweden first. That is because they have focused on safety in their marketing.

If you manufacture or market products as opposed to services, you can use your products to do alchemy for you. You do this by placing them where they will reinforce their brand personality and, perhaps, generate demand. For instance, an up-market independent bakery might provide bread rolls for a fund-raising barbecue. People attending the barbecue are made aware of the sponsorship through the promotional print. Not only do they form a favourable impression of the bakery, but they have an opportunity to sample the products as well. Other examples of product alchemy include the following.

DIY shop gives paint to local scout group to redecorate their scout hut	Parents are more likely to patronise the shop, particularly if a sign acknowledges the gift
Garden centre gives trees to public park	Provides free advertising all year round
Confectionery maker gives chocolate bars to every runner in marathon	Press coverage publicises association with sporting achievement

Brand alchemy

If your organisation works in a business-to-business environment, or perhaps provides services rather than products, you can use your brand values instead. The same rules apply; you must endeavour to do alchemy where your commercial audience are most likely to spot it. Many trade associations have their own charities that exist to help members at times of trauma. These are usually supported financially by members. There are often opportunities here for alchemy, but using your staff time and other resources, rather than cash. Other members of the association, perhaps also your customers, recognise your involvement and are more likely to use your services.

Consider now your product or service. Are there opportunities to place your brand where it can do alchemy for you?

Check-list	Example
Establish your brand characteristics	Pet insurance sold over the internet.
Identify opportunity for brand alchemy	Host 'lost pets' website.
Make it happen	Set up and promote site, using staff volunteers. Everyone becomes aware that you care for pets.

Ready-made alchemy

Many of the larger charities offer ready-made alchemy solutions. They have recognised that not everyone has the time or ingenuity to devise their own programmes. In their defence, it must be said that you can gain a very good payback from involvement in national campaigns. A good example is a printer who would organise a sponsored gym session for all of its staff every December to raise money for a national children's charity campaign. Every customer, past and present, would be contacted and cajoled into sponsoring the activity. Many were inclined to do so because the cause was well-known and respected. The printer gained:

- Press publicity because they raised a lot of money
- A team-building opportunity because everyone joined in and enjoyed the day
- Tangible support from customers, many of whom also gave the company an order
- An opportunity to benefit from the nationally respected charity's image

You will often see advertisements placed by charities to attract individuals to, for example, run in the London marathon. The benefit for the charity is that runners raise sponsorship money and wear branded t-shirts during the race. As an alchemist, you could go one better and enter a company team, wearing your corporate colours alongside those of the good cause.

Take a fresh look at your Sunday paper. You will probably find plenty of invitations to get involved in national campaigns. Look closer and you will see opportunities to change things slightly so that you can be recognised as an innovative alchemist. Try it and see.

Learning in the voluntary sector

As with education, there are countless opportunities for you and your staff to broaden their horizons and develop new skills through involvement in the voluntary sector. There is a growing need for business skills in not-for-profit organisations. Again, in common with education, the language and terminology is different. It could be argued that there are more opportunities for self-development alchemy in the voluntary sector because the range of organisations is so diverse. You can also choose to work with organisations whose sphere of activity interests you. This makes volunteering even more interesting. Let us look at some examples and how they might fit into your company training plan.

Charity need	Opportunity	Suitable for
Local committee role	Develop team-working skills	Junior managers
Trustee of local charity	Develop strategic skills	Middle managers
Trustee of national charity	Widen experience and build network	Board members

There are also all of the opportunities that we have already discussed and that you may have started to practise. These include the chance to share training resources with a local charity, explore mentoring relationships and much more.

You can also link this activity to areas of personal interest, both for you and your employees. It is often said that most businesses have within their workforce, skills and expertise they are not aware of. Why not use this exercise as your opportunity to audit your company's skills, focusing particularly on out of work interests?

How to entertain your customers for free

This is a personal favourite, and this use of alchemy could perhaps be exploited as a commercial opportunity. An example of this alchemy was used by a business that sold soil and peat to golf courses. The business was quite unsophisticated and very profitable. This is what they did.

One summer the business decided to stage a large barbecue in their yard and to entertain all of their customers, suppliers and friends. They also wanted to invite people who were not yet customers. The trouble was, they had nothing new to say or show, so could not offer the usual 'product launch' event. In fact, there really was little reason for the barbecue, other than the business owner's desire to strengthen contact with the company's audience. The moment of true alchemy was when the owner decided to make the event a fund-raiser for a local children's hospice.

Other local businesses donated food and drink, a local band offered to entertain his guests and everyone who attended purchased a ticket because they were eager to support the hospice too. The result was a very successful evening which was well attended, raised more than £1,000 for the hospice and cost the host nothing.

How to do it

You can see from the above example that it is quite easy to entertain your clients for nothing while, at the same time, supporting a worthy cause. As with any alchemy, the better the fit, the better the result. For instance, my own company wanted to organise a coach trip to the NEC Motor Show to do some client bonding. Clients might have been reluctant to pay, had we not decided to donate our profits from the day to the Disabled Drivers Association. Not only did we sell every seat, we also persuaded local motor dealers to give us prizes which we raffled on the coach. We had a superb day out with our clients and appeared in our local paper presenting a cheque for £350 to the charity. To make this happen for you, you need to do the following.

Plan	Exactly what do you want to achieve and with who? What good cause is appropriate and will add value?
Involve	Find others to share the project. Their guests might be your prospects! Tenants in a serviced office building might decide to organise a collective event.
Link	Fund-raising is more effective if linked to a specific appeal. Set a target with your chosen charity.
Deliver	Make the event a success. Involve a local PR firm if you do not feel confident enough to organise it yourself.

Publicise	Write to everyone who attended to thank them for their contribution. Enclose a copy of your press release and photo of the presentation to the charity.
Repeat	Seek ideas from all who came for next year's event!

Summary

Let us end this day by reflecting on what we have covered. We have discovered that the voluntary sector is vast. It even includes the many religious groups we have in the UK. For some businesses, particularly those working with sections of our population where religion is important, a church project might present powerful alchemy opportunities.

We have looked at how you can make quite a big difference to a small project by getting your staff involved. Remember too that charities usually pay low wages and attract staff who are very caring, but perhaps may not have benefited from extensive training and development programmes. Your staff will find that they have plenty of skills and experience that they can share. This boosts self-esteem and often helps people to see just how lucky they are to be working or living where and as they are.

In common with all forms of alchemy, we have recognised that the more you put in, the more you will get out. In other words, if the project is your idea, it will be tailored to meet your needs first. There is nothing wrong with this, providing that others benefit too.

Using other people's money to achieve your business goals

This week we have looked at how we can develop alchemy using other organisations to add value and reduce, or even eliminate, cost. Today, as the week draws to a close, we confront the issue of funding head on. Our focus has been to avoid paying out hard cash, although at times spending money cannot be avoided. We shall now look at how to make sure that as much as possible of what you spend is actually someone else's money!

There are many people who will claim to be able to help you access grant funding for your business. Many of them do no more than you can do yourself and a few are downright rogues! As an alchemist, you can create your own funding opportunities. Here are the topics that we will cover today:

- Why is there public funding for businesses?
- How to present your needs in an appealing way
- Getting noticed and getting your share
- Succeeding with others
- Putting something back

Before we start, here are a few hard facts about public money. First, it is of course your money. Governments collect taxes and then use the money to benefit the people it governs. Second, there are stringent audit processes that account for public expenditure. This means that public budget holders need to be confident that your idea is both robust and will add value before they invest.

Why is there public funding?

This is not a textbook about economics, but you do need to appreciate some of the basic facts about how public money is spent. Perhaps it is more important to understand that government investment in one area can deliver massive savings in another. One of the basic tenets of 'joined-up' government is the adoption of a holistic view of expenditure. The alternative would be that each department budgets without recognising the contribution that another can make. You could call this idea of being joined-up government alchemy!

The competitive dimension

There is of course another dimension. Economically, the UK is not isolated, it both imports and exports products and services. The more competitive our businesses become, the better the balance of trade. Much of the DTI's focus is on helping us to compete better in world markets. This is why the DTI runs trade missions and develops programmes to make our businesses more efficient.

Other government departments focus on the skills agenda, encouraging us to embrace the concept of 'lifelong learning', and others endeavour to create an infrastructure of transport, health and education that supports our national vision. The European government also has a role to play, taking money from affluent areas and investing it in developing the less well off areas. Some streams of European money can be drawn down in all areas of the UK.

What does all this mean to the business alchemist? Well, not surprisingly when you actually break those governmental budgets down, there is not enough to go round. What we can do as alchemists is to make sure that when this money is handed out, we are towards the front of the queue. The following, in general terms, is what public budget holders are looking for.

Added value	For example, how many new jobs will you create?
On time	Your projects have to run to timetable, not over-run
Additionality	Public money has to create something new, not simply replace what would have happened anyway
Case studies	The best projects can be used to illustrate success
Ethical	Some business types are not deemed ethical places to invest public money

Preparing to attract public money

Clearly you need to be prepared to 'toe the line' and deliver the kind of results that can be hailed as examples of good practice and sound investment. What sort of projects will attract support? There are three basic types of public funding available to businesses.

Knowledge	Usually DTI funded and often 'branded initiatives' that deliver aspects of good working practice. Best accessed via the Business Link network. There is a Business Link in every English county and equivalents in Scotland, Wales and Northern Ireland.
Skill	Subsidised learning for employees. Emanates from the DfES (Department for Education and Skills) and Europe, and usually accessed through local outlets of the Learning and Skills Council.
Infrastructure	From investment in business incubators to grants for converting redundant farm buildings. Opportunities best identified via the economic development unit of your local authority.

You also need to appreciate that there is often competition for the limited budgets available.

How to get noticed

In most cases there is not enough money to invest in every possible project or business. What is more, when these initiatives are structured, there are targets to achieve. These targets will cover such things as where you are based, the gender and race of those the project will help, how many people are involved and the expected life of the project.

Make sure that your project is written in such a way that it meets your target funders criteria.

Preparing your bid

To attract funding for your business you need to carry out the following, considering in particular the points above.

Have a strong business argument for what you want to achieve:

- Does it create new jobs?
- Will other businesses benefit? (your suppliers, for example)
- How horrible is the alternative? (factory closure for example)

Make contact with and seek advice from the appropriate organisation

- As an alchemist, you need to maintain dialogue with budget holders and those who influence them.
- Spend time studying support agency and governmental websites. Understand what the initiatives are.

Structure your proposition to deliver the outcomes that your funder is seeking:

- Proposals for funding need to focus on delivering what the money is designed for, not what your business plan seeks to achieve.

> Build a reputation for doing what you say you are going to do:
>
> - Invest time and effort in getting known as someone who delivers.
> - Get involved in local consultation groups and always attend funders' events.

Remember that the budget holders at the various organisations who are managing the projects will want you to succeed. The more competition they can attract for funding and the better quality the bids, the better value they achieve. Many organisations hold workshops for people preparing bids for European money because the process itself is complex. While they will not write your bid or proposal for you, always remember that the budget holding organisation wants to help you win. We have not talked about consultants yet, but here, perhaps for the first time, is an area where an independent business consultant could really help you.

Some simple examples

We have talked a great deal about the theory of winning external funding for your business. That is in part because you need to understand the mechanism before you can operate the machine. It is also because the rules are always changing. However, we can illustrate what can be achieved with a mini case study. Everything that this company does has been achieved in the recent past. It may not always be achievable tomorrow, but it still makes the point.

Business stage	Project	Funding won
Start up	• Grant for consultancy won from local council • Free business training from Enterprise Agency	£400 grant Worth £2000
Employs people	• Free management training from Business Link • Free consultancy to help achieve Investors in People • Free NVQ programme for staff members under 25 years	Worth £2000 Worth £1500 £1000 each
Win new business	• Free business diagnostic from Business Link • 50 per cent grant towards approved marketing programme	Worth £2500 £5000 grant
Improve quality	• Free workshops to help achieve ISO9001 • Free consultancy to achieve Business Excellence (European funded, delivered by an industry network)	Worth £3000 Worth £5000
Develop new product	• DTI SMART award to cover a feasibility study into a new product. There must be a risk of failure and, usually, new technology should result	£45,000 max

You can now see what can be achieved. Let us look at how we can improve your chances of success.

Two heads are better than one

Now that you are getting interested in this form of alchemy, we can introduce the missing element; other businesses. We have said throughout that you can achieve so much more if you work with others. Remember that, while you are competing for limited funds of grant money, you are not competing in the conventional sense. It is not like commercial competition where you feel the need to remove a rival from the field of play. In reality, if you collaborate with similar companies to your own, you will be able to create a far more appealing proposition. At a national level, trade associations often succeed in winning funding for training and development across their industry.

This may be a good time to tell you that, not surprisingly, much public money is spent on recruiting and managing projects reducing the cash available to help people and businesses to succeed. Can you see now why it is helpful to collaborate with others? Here are some benefits of working together:

- You stand a far better chance of winning funding
- You will also learn from your collaborators
- There will be other opportunities for alchemy that result from the liaison
- There is more scope to tailor the project to your needs because it will be larger

Making it happen

As an alchemist, you need to take the initiative and lead your collaborative project to success. Some informal sounding out of other businesses in your area or business sector is a good place to start. You need to be sure of the need and of your popularity before getting too involved, otherwise there is a danger of looking foolish. Here is a check-list of the processes you need to follow.

Research opportunities	Find out what funding is around by talking with and taking an interest in local support organisations.
Build a network	Recruit others to join you, name your network and develop some shared vision. Your initial research will have established a need.
Introduce funder	Invite your target funder to meet and speak to your group. This will be both powerful and very helpful.
Ask funder to detail their priorities	This makes sure that you aim for what is easiest to achieve. Remember, the funder's agenda comes first!
Put together your proposal	If unsure, use a consultant to write your bid. Do not be afraid to show the funder 'drafts' and seek feedback. This will keep them involved and help you to prepare something that wins support.

Keep network 'on board'	Ensure that you keep communicating with and involving your collaborators. They will quickly lose interest if not refreshed with enthusiasm often.
Win support	At this point publicise your success and attract enquiries from more participants. This gives you choice and makes succeeding easier.
Deliver project	Now you can make it happen and keep your funder involved at every stage. You have done alchemy!

Putting something back

By now, you are an experienced alchemist and have started to help those responsible for public expenditure to spend it more wisely and effectively. Your own business will be known as a leader and, hopefully, all of this 'good practice' is beginning to reflect in your organisation's performance. In other words, you are delivering the growth that your business plan demands. Now it is time to put something back and repay the investment made in you and your business. You will not be surprised to learn that the activities we are about to propose enable even more business alchemy to take place. The table overleaf explains this.

Activity	What is involved	Alchemy
Becomes a business case study	Feature in the marketing of government initiatives as a success story	Provides free marketing for your business
Host 'best practice' visits	Other companies visit you to see how you did it (you can of course veto direct competitors)	You learn from your visitors, build your network and often recruit new collaborators
Speak at 'best practice' conferences	You share your experience with potentially large business audiences	Your audience will contain potential new suppliers, customers and employees
Join the board of a business support organisation	You have become a champion and are shaping support strategies	The experience helps with your professional development

Summary

Well, you have been working hard and, in truth, we have much to cover tomorrow in pulling together all that we have discussed so far. We can conclude our tour of public funding opportunities with an exercise to ensure that you have followed the story so far and feel confident enough to try this very important form of alchemy.

- Make a list of your business goals for the next 2 years – this will focus your mind.
- Make a list of all the businesses you can think of that could 'share your journey'.
- Write on the list when (if ever) you last met your opposite numbers in those businesses.
- Open your diary, pick up the phone and arrange some meetings. Remember, one of the best excuses for meeting is to discuss a third company.

When you have done this, you are on the way to success.

Bringing it all together

You will have realised that there are opportunities for alchemy in almost every walk of life. Our focus here is to use alchemy to benefit our organisations and careers. In fact, organisation and career are usually inextricably linked. It is only by growing your company, that you can continue to grow your career. We have to constantly learn, and apply that learning, to grow the business.

Today is our last day together and you have worked hard to consider how you can apply alchemy in your business. We shall now focus on building an 'alchemy plan' for our business:

- Planning the game
- Choosing the players
- Making it happen
- Measuring success

Planning the game

We talked on Sunday about the importance of planning. Everyone has to know what they want to achieve personally before they can really plan career or business goals. You also need to think through the goals you have set yourself. Look back to any notes you may have made. What are the things you really want to achieve? Many people use financial targets as goals, but remember that money is only a means to an end; no one ever chose to spend their time sitting in a bank! Think about your goals in the following terms.

Where	Where do you want to spend your time? Visualise your ideal work/home environments. Do not forget holiday dreams.
What	What do you want to do with your time? You are bright and will not want to simply switch off and watch the waves on a beach. List the activities you want to indulge in.
Who	Who do you want to spend time with? You may have a partner – are your respective goals compatible? Think too about who you want to work with, socialise with, perhaps even help.
When	When do you plan to get to your destination? Often your ability to visualise far into the future depends on your age now. Set milestones to mark your progress and review them monthly.
How	If you have answered the above questions honestly and discussed your goals with your life partner, the 'how' is easy. You will intuitively know what you have to do. Alchemy can help you do it faster!

Choosing the players

This part is often the hardest because the unskilled alchemist will tend to select the most obvious people to work with. Colleagues, friends and neighbours. Remember, though, that there are more than 300 million people living in Europe alone. You only know a few of them. Inevitably, the people who will make the biggest difference are those you have yet to meet. This is why we brushed up on our networking skills earlier in the week.

The other thing you have to do is to get noticed. You have to stand out from the crowd. We live in a crowded country, in a crowded world. Be different. Alchemy is perhaps the best way to be different and one of the best ways to meet new people. Here are some advanced techniques for building your network.

Diversity	Make sure you mix the people from the different sectors we have visited. They will link in other ways, keeping alchemy fresh.
Research	Always take the time to find out as much as you can about a person, their role and their goals before rushing to meet them.
Give before taking	Meet their needs before seeking help in meeting yours. For alchemy to work, all must benefit. Help the other person first and you will get more back from them and their contacts.
Keep in the centre	Always make sure that you remain the broker. Introduce people from different sectors and benefit from their synergy.

Making it happen

We have already talked about how to make it happen. Crucial to your success will be your willingness to learn and to start with small 'low risk' projects. Get yourself known as the person who makes things happen. Others will then start to want you in their networks.

We talked earlier about creating a network that enables a number of alchemy projects to follow each other. This can be a key component in your success. Remember that running a network is rather like producing a company or community newsletter. To start with, everyone wants to help and everyone has lots of ideas. After a while, most lose interest and the project flounders. As an alchemist, you must be constantly seeking out new ideas to add vigour to your network. If you can keep your key partners and collaborators excited, they will keep working. Do not leave it to chance.

Measuring success

You may know that PR agencies usually measure their
success by the extent of press coverage they win for their
clients. They compare their fee for the work with what it
would have cost their client to buy that same space for
advertising. It gives a very good measure of performance.

As an alchemist, you too will have to constantly remind
people of the value you have added. While by no means as
straightforward as the PR example, the same technique can
be used to measure your success. This is how to do it.

Activity	What took place? How many people? What is the gain worth?
Alternative	How else could you have achieved the same goal?
Value	Compare gain with the actual cost and the cost of the alternative.
Share	Make sure your participants know how lucky they are. Make sure that you pick up on any ideas that can make you more successful next time.
Celebrate	People tend to forget good news. Remind them with a party. Remember to use the technique we covered earlier to make sure that the party itself is an example of alchemy.

So now you are an alchemist

Congratulations. You have completed the book and taken part in exploring how alchemy can make your life better. To get on in any walk of life, you have to engage with and influence other people. Success is really no more complicated than that. Remember:

- Set goals

- Explore opportunities

- Involve others

- Make it happen